I0151369

Surface Textures

poems by

Heidi Hemmer

Finishing Line Press
Georgetown, Kentucky

Surface Textures

ACKNOWLEDGMENTS

The Best Part of Waking Up: *FishFood Magazine*, July 2018
Extremity: *Black Fox Literary Magazine*, August 2017
Naked and Alive: *Nude Bruce Review*, April 2017
Surface Textures: *Oddball Magazine*, September 2016
The Great Minnesota Commute: *The Talking Stick*, September 2014
Picking Trees Bark: *The Talking Stick*, September 2013
Unemployment: *The Southwest Journal*, June 2012

Publisher: Leah Maines
Editor: Christen Kincaid
Cover Art: Cheryl Wold
Author Photo and Design: Jeff Fuller

Printed in the USA on acid-free paper.
Order online: www.finishinglinepress.com
also available on amazon.com

Author inquiries and mail orders:
Finishing Line Press
P. O. Box 1626
Georgetown, Kentucky 40324
U. S. A.

Table of Contents

Part 1: Nature

Extremity

Millie's hands have spent days in the sun
harvesting the dry raspberries.
She has forgotten countless
times to apply sunscreen to her hands,
and they have aged: bony, wrinkly, and tan.

Millie picks the raspberries for the last time
this season and bathes them for eating.
The cold water relieves the pain in her joints,
her fingers free for a few moments.

She pops a couple in her mouth, the
juiciness reminds her of life's sweetness.
Millie will mow the plants to the ground,
an easy death before winter.

Naked and Alive

Burgundy peeks out
like a glass of wine
after a hard day's work. Trees
turn, no longer burdened with
heavy loads, stand with
exposed souls, waiting
for first frost to take the edge off.

With bare branches,
                    they
                              live.

The North Shore at Night

Lake Superior whispers white,
beneath the wind,
sea smoke rising.
The American Carrier
skates across the lake,
awaiting her axel.
The moon illuminates the
black, boulders caressing
twilight with firm hands.
The trees admire the beauty
within the cold, covered in
icicles, baring bones.

The Ram

The Highline Trail, dusted
by dew, pebbles, and
sneakers, leads hikers
to Logan's Pass.
Downhill,
below the chaos—
life in its natural form.

A ram grazes overgrown
grass, as his herd
rests on rocks, tired from
the mountain beating sun.
Soon, the mob balances the rocks
like ballet dancers to unite

with their leader. The ram rubs
his buttocks against the Douglas Fir
one sniffs a Glacier's Lily,
while another sharpens
his horns for the fight tonight.

The Great Minnesota Winter Commute

I. *The Car Commuter*

A dead snowman covers your windshield. You don't slip on the mittens your mother gave you, you are tough. You put the key in ignition, while you scrap the car. Sitting out in negative six degree weather, Mr. Dodge shudders and moans. The dark morning reminds you how much you miss summer. You drive down I-94. There has been an accident. Why is it that no one knows how to drive in winter, but you? Cars try to budge, but you are riding bumper to bumper. Not even the hill billy pick up truck from Cottage Grove bothers you. You arrive to work forty five minutes late. You take off your slushy boots and slip into your heels. You put your brown bagged lunch away in the bipolar fridge (sometimes it freezes your soda, sometimes it melts your lean cuisine). You reach into your bag for your laptop (all the work you did over the weekend) and realize it is not there.

II. *The Bus Commuter*

At six below, you wait at the bus stop for the 4P to downtown. The usual three wait with you; the guy with the long pony tail who enjoys comics, the blonde with curly hair who you see everywhere but never acknowledges you or says hi, and the emo punk teenager who always lights a cigarette and smokes it in depressing way. The cold air attacks your nostrils freezing the hair and the boogers, making your nose run. You push up your scarf to cover your nose and mouth, but then it fogs your glasses. You walk back and forth in a circle, just so you can feel something. You look down the road for the 4P, 4P, 4P, 4P. The bus crawls stop by stop. The roads are bad. The traffic is bad and there has been a bad accident. Forty five minutes late, you take off your slushy boots and slip into your heels. You put your lunch away in the bipolar fridge (sometimes it freezes your soda, sometimes it melts your lean cuisine). You reach into your bag for your laptop and realize it is not there.

Cancun, Mexico, January 2014

Broken seashells
    crawl between my toes,
a cool breeze soothes the sunburn,
     I taste salt.
Waves splash against each other
    like children on a merry go round.

  Chatter from all different languages
      swirl
through the air.
     I have forgotten which country I claim.

  I walk into the water.
     The power
moving my body as it wishes,
     riding each wave like a pelican.

Picking Tree's Bark

The willow
sweeps back and forth
massaging the air
       in the rough wind.
My hair snaggles, goosebumps
  appear on my arms.
 The grass
prickles
   below. Squirrels watch me
walk by.

 Your
face is in
that tree. Silky smooth dark complexion,
Cheshire cat smile.
      Even that tree has a
      big forehead.

I wrap my arms around the trunk,
picking off bark,
tears start to
    fall.
    The squirrels shake their heads and continue
to gather nuts.

West Coast Swing: Part One

We drive a curved road where
        ocean meets mountains.
 A breathtaking view
        even the driver takes a peak.
Tourists travel in large vans stuffed
of children eating Skittles.

 View spots are infested with
        people who watch the waves crash
against the splintered rocks
        and admire the Bixby Bridge.

Soon the road crowds with Redwoods,
        reaching for the sky
my head tries to find the ending,
        like Jack and his beanstalk.

The sun sets as darkness
        enters the forest, speeding my
heartbeat, which speeds the car.
        to our rustic, modern cabin.

A fireplace patio
        welcomes us, a slit screen
to stars of the night sky.
        The cool breeze pecks at my
cheeks, he reaches for my hand.
        We toast our wine glasses,
underneath the canvas, laughing and smiling.

He caresses my face and
        spills
            red
                wine
                    on
                        my
                            dress!

West Coast Swing: Part Two

We leave our hotel early to join
strangers on a party bus to Wine Country.
We cruise pass the homeless man with a pan
for donations, several Walgreens, and
businessmen on cell phones to reach Union Square.

The bus salutes us with energy, chatter, dry bagels.
Our chauffeur: a comedian with a Middle Eastern accent.

Jacuzzi Winery, to sample wine and olives.
The New Yorkers rude, insulting the liquid,
as well as the tender. I am proud to say I am a Midwest girl.
We stroll the courtyard, admiring the vines,
and each other. My husband takes too many pictures
—statues, selfies, and sweetness.

Back on the bus, the crowd is drunk dancing to
ACDC's "Back in Black". It isn't even noon yet.

Three Labs Winery greets the guests.
We taste chocolate, wine and the mountain view.
The chauffer transforms to a chef, a picnic at Madonna estate.
Enchanted by the Butler's friend demonstration
(or perhaps too much alcohol)
we buy an opener for keepsake. I am still not sure how to use it.

We pack on the bus one last time. Soon, the
tourists are sleeping, one drooling, with her mouth wide open.

Cabin Sounds

At 1:14am, I hear
the fluttering of the June bug
on the moth eaten screen,
crickets clicking,
loons swooning,
a train choo chooing,
neighbors cackling over
beers and bonfire, and
the raccoon trying to open
a mouse trap.

My husband snores.

Runners' Nod

Trees stare into the sky,
        dogs bark at our speed, feet
stomp sidewalk in dark summer parks.
        Sweat drips, sunglasses slip,
untied shoestrings trip,
        our limbs move muscles—
puppets on drugs.
        Along the Mississippi Boulevard,
we emerge like weeds,
        passing pedestrians, skaters, and bikes.

Runners: Signal the code.
        Unite, together, we fly!

Kinda Fun

Poets loiter the coffee shop,
observing unsatisfactory pick up lines,
wanna be bikers bragging
about their motorcycles
and discussing the pros and cons
of stealing street flower pots.

It's like high school again. Standing
outside, not cool enough to
be invited inside, but not dumb
enough to walk in.

Part Two: Neuroses

Surface Textures

Under our mattress of memory foam,
I found your suicide note.
Every night, I turned and tossed
Countless times,

I stripped the bedsheets
for wash, then tightly tucked
under the mattress;
a chore concluded.

I shoved unwanted wall art,
useless boxes underneath,
our cat buried between the junk,
never noticing the note.

You wrote in Helvetica,
a robust vocabulary,
twenty four pound paper with
a perfect woven finish.

I now sleep on the floor, clawing carpet.

The Best Part of Waking Up

The days go into
      the moon, who
rests gently against the galaxy.

As the moon drifts
      to slumber, I stare
at the ceiling, concentrating on

madness, energy, and blackness.
      The arms of the alarm
clock turn quickly from evening,

mid morning, dawn. Rudely,
      screams as I stare
at the texture of whiteness.

My sleepless body aches for
      rest, eyes like
the end of a boxing match.

Normal people would
      call in sick.
I pour a cup of coffee.

Through the Walls

Glass breaks against
the brick wall, books fall off the shelves,
hands shatter the mirror.

I could hear *you* beat her through the walls.

The smell of Black Velvet, the lights
going out, the Siamese cat
bolts up the stairs.

I could hear *you* beat her through the walls.

Screams and bruises fill the air, black
eyes with cuts, and tank tops
splattered with blood.

I could hear *you* beat her through the walls.

Hairs stick up on my tattered teddy bear,
goose bumps shiver my nightgown,
our sobs unnoticed.

Counting Sheep

The sheep are counting the
humans until they are dead.

The dealers count the addicted,
after the president declared
war on drugs, wanting to be
inflicted for a night in a vacant,
boarded building, where mattresses
lie in rat afflicted halls.

The drunks count on friends
Jim, Jack, Ron and the Captain
to help bend with pretty
girls in a night club, but
instead end up on the ground
dancing with beetles.

The gamblers count on sight
enduring night after night
on torn red stools
in front of noisy slots that light,
waiting for the green.

The sheep graze the future
until it is too late.

Delectable Daisy

Stars in the sky,
       we lie next
to each other, holding hands, hearts
       and time.

Manga eyes, Russian red
       lips and cheeks
My head spins as I caress curves,
       actionable items and verbs

we move together like water
       in waves, up and
down, never to drown.

Her nipples are pointy
       and hard, like
me knee deep, never asleep

she moves me to heights
       so tight
in between, hard to breathe.

Late at night, beside my wife
       I dream of Daisy.
I never should have told her

I am married.

Tavis

In Memory of Tavis Leaf

Newports and Parliaments,
the parking lot,
cold wind biting our cheeks
as we exhale, escaping
for just a moment, that
moment, together, we are

free.

Unemployment

You sit around, picking your nose
watching reality TV shows. I

forget which one as they are all
the same. You open a keystone light

and put your feet up on the end
table burned with cigarette holes

bumpy with mumps. You laugh
as one of the girls falls down drunk,

squirting beer all over the mud stained
rug. Your girlfriend sits next to you

lighting a Basic light, itching her
fat roll. The damn dog, covered

in loneliness, whimpers in her filth
next to the motionless ball. Her sounds

disappear quicker than the government
checks. Ramon noodles and dust fill the

cupboards. Trash fills the studio apartment
eating the walls, it becomes décor.

The sun spits in the window. You squint
outside, and shut the broken blinds.

As you pour the Black Velvet, you
realize it doesn't get any better than this.

Box Cutter

A puddle lies
on the bathroom floor
next to
the cigarette burn
concealed with whiteout.

The redness
trickles down
my unshaven legs,
evil
spewing out
like booze in a
broken whiskey bottle.

I sit and stare at
the bathroom wall,
covered with art.
Socks and long sleeves,
all black, no skirts,
now better.

With a smile on my face,
I get back to work.

Knots on a Rope

Lily ties
      a hammock,
between
      two bruised trees,
near the Lake of the Isles.

Her hideaway spot,
      she lights a cigarette
staring at ducks
      free on water.

If Lily was
      a duck, she
could escape
      when winter
chills her body.

Lily swings in the
      hammock, the gust
nips her cheek,
      she plans to fly,
hanging
      between
those two bruised trees.

A Portrait in Smoke

The curtains,
half open, sunshine
taps the window.
Cigarette smoke
suffocates the white walls,
with picked off paint chips.
Shag carpet
crawls with cat hair,
half-eaten Cheerios.
The chair, worn and tired,
sits with two little girls—
dirty hands, puffy eyes,
bruised legs, reading about
princesses. They don't know
the future.

Black Lace Dress

I drive past the cemetery
where mother is buried
beneath the
grass grieving silence,
left alone
in her black lace dress
the one dad didn't
want her to buy.
Her diamond
stuck on her
knobby finger
clings to her
marriage;
a good catholic.
I wonder if
Dad ever
thinks of her
anymore—
decorating the
Christmas tree with
child made ornaments,
dancing in the
passenger seat,
reading
on our porch,
rocking
back and forth
to sunlight.

Or if he is too busy fucking Francine.
They say mother died of cancer, but
I know what killed her.

Shadow People

The hairs of your arm stick up into the
see-your-own breath weather
but not because of chilled air.

Tingly, light headed
you tread the ice covered sidewalks,
careful not to step on the cracks
without looking back.

Lock the doors,
perhaps triple-check,
but you never escape your fear.

Gunner

He stumbles streets, listens
to lamp light, puffs his
cigarette with a nicotine patch
on his right shoulder. He wears
a red leather jacket,
rips under the pocket, hair
slicked back black.
Pupils dilated as the moon,
stars smile- he avoids
the sidewalk cracks,
smells moss on the rocks,
soil sprinkled with worms.
He stares at a fallen maple leaf,
the perfect five lobe shape-
veins protrude, colors change
the beauty he never saw.

We Never Left the Hotel Room

Five star, fancy hotel.
The bathroom in
          middle of the suite,
see through glass, with two
shower heads. We never felt so clean.

Ophelia

Auburn
hair spills
into the water,
swallowing
her pale face.
Violets
choke her neck,
roses
swim softly,
poppies
wait for death.

A robin
listens—
Ophelia
sings songs
of joy turn to
confusion.
Her embroidered
silver dress
plunges
her deep
into madness—
eyes wide open.

The broken
      willow
           opens her branches,
          Ophelia's limbs
              beg for mercy.

Heidi Hemmer has been writing and publishing poetry for over fifteen years. Heidi's poetry utilizes visceral imagery, dark humor, and a forlorn wistfulness to start conversations about nature's inherent beauty, mental illness, and drug abuse. She has been published in the *Wild Leaf Press, The Southwest Journal, The Talking Stick Journal, OddballMagazine, Nude Bruce Journal, The Black Fox Literary Magazine,* and *Fish Food Magazine.*

Beyond her poetry, Heidi Hemmer also writes and designs corporate learning and development curriculum and provides senior thought-leadership in her professional field. She has a master of arts in organizational psychology. Heidi currently lives in the bone chilling cold of Saint Paul, Minnesota, with her husband and Instagram celebrity cat, @BanditTorpedo